HIDE & SEEK | SYDNEY

GW00482219

HIDE & SEEK | SYDNEY

contents

004 / hit the streets

026 / treasure trove

048 / feeling peckish?

070 / night owl

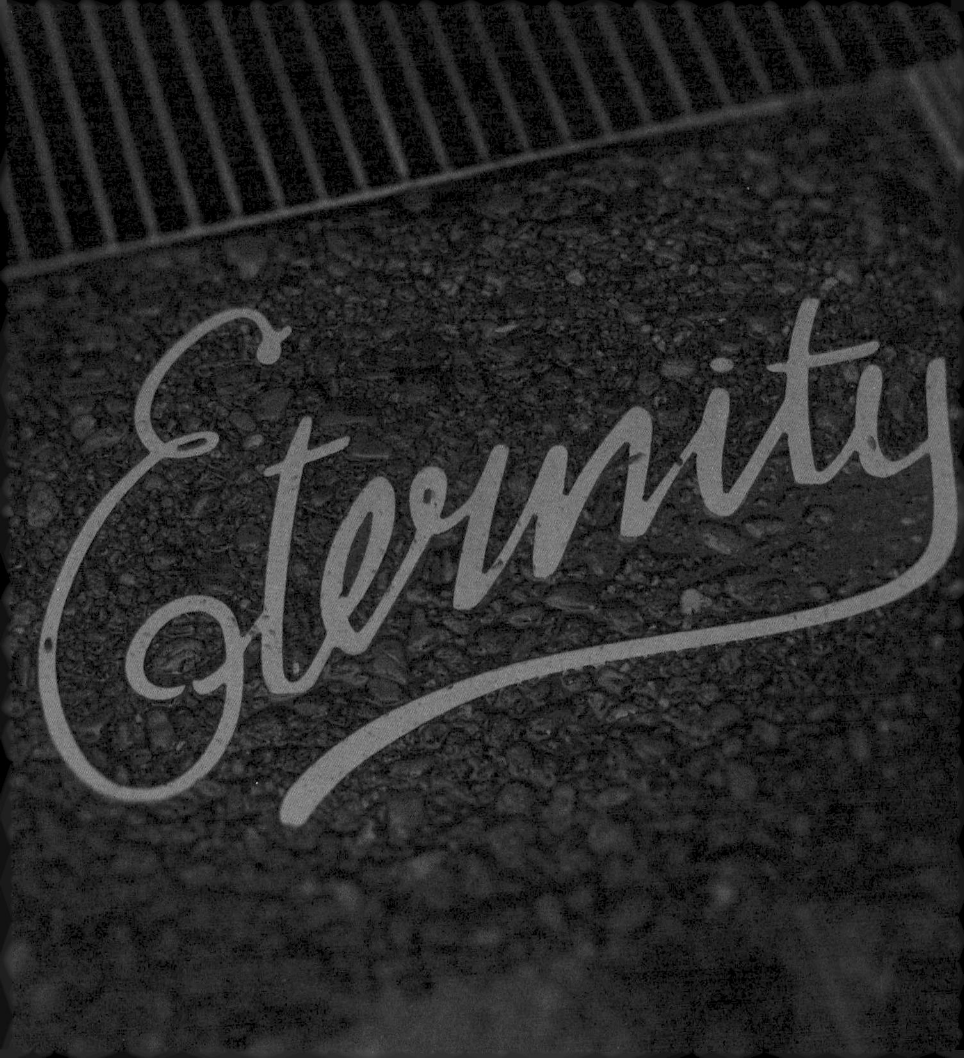
Eternity

READY-SET-GO | SYDNEY

Sydney is Australia's glittering city with more style and flair than Carrie Bradshaw's shoe collection. Sun, surf, beaches, iconic locations, a load of tourist attractions, top restaurants and swanky bars – this city has got it all. But then there's the persistent rumour that a bouncer will size up your outfit at every Sydney nightclub and everything's just a tad more expensive than anywhere else in the country. So, where does that leave the vast majority of us who can't afford to spend a small fortune on anything, let alone shoes? The answer is that there's a lot more to Sydney than just VIP-only clubs and second mortgage–sized price tags. You just need to know where to go, which is where this handy little guide comes in.

Hide & Seek Sydney is for all Sydneysiders, interstate travellers and overseas visitors who want to experience another side of what Sydney has to offer. We've done our best to identify 40 of the most interesting and unique places, both in the city centre and inner suburbs. The book is divided into four, colour-coded chapters packed with ideas to help you fill your day, your bag, your stomach and your ears: **Hit the Streets** (ten places to go or things to do once you've seen the Sydney Opera House and have been to Bondi); **Treasure Trove** (ten unique shopping experiences that'll make you wonder why you bother with brand stores); **Feeling Peckish?** (ten ways to fill that hole and sample Sydney's eclectic range of eateries); **Night Owl** (ten bars, clubs and music venues to get you glowing in the dark as you mingle, dance or groove the night away). There's something for everyone here, no matter what your tastes or interests. And, in all cases, we've tried to make sure that you won't need a platinum Amex card or a designer wardrobe just to get through the front door.

I'd like to say thank you to the freelancers whose contributions have made *Hide & Seek Sydney* possible: to Erika Budiman for her incredible design and excellent photographs, to KJ Eyre for her editorial expertise, and to our in-house cartographer Emily Maffei for her funky maps. Thanks also to the amazing team of in-the-know Sydneysiders who researched and wrote the reviews with such enthusiasm and dedication.

Finally, if you find somewhere hidden in Sydney that you think others should seek out, please send us an email at **info@exploreaustralia.net.au**. Otherwise, there are a couple of blank pages at the back of the book for you to record your own discoveries as you explore this charismatic and colourful city.

Cheers,
Melissa Krafchek | Editor

about the writers

NICK DENT
Born in Brisbane, Nick has lived in inner-city Sydney for ten years and loves its combination of sunshine, culture and great food. His day job is arts, film and museums editor of essential entertainment guide *Time Out Sydney* and he has written extensively about the city for *City Weekly*, *SX*, *Black+White* and *Blue* magazines. He lives within 3 min walk of six of Sydney's finest pubs, but that's just a coincidence.

JOANNA BOUNDS
Born in the UK, Joanna arrived in Sydney at the height of Mardi Gras madness in 1999, falling headfirst into the decadent delights of the city, before being offered a job at *Vogue Australia* while sunning herself on Bondi beach. Since becoming a managing editor, and shopping and style writer for *The Sydney Morning Herald*, she likes to think she has the lowdown on all of Sydney's highlights.

DENBY WELLER
Hailing from Queensland, Denby first discovered Sydney on a family holiday at age eight. Declaring at once that she would one day live here, she made good on her promise ten years later, and the affair has lasted. When she's not directing films or penning screenplays, Denby can be found cruising the streets of her beloved city on her motorbike, or engaging in the delightfully endless search for The Perfect Coffee.

DANIEL BISHTON
Growing up in Sydney's leafy north shore, Daniel was drawn to the sparkling grime of the inner west at the tender age of 13. While finishing off his Masters in Journalism at UTS, he helps present the infamous, infrequent *Rock 'n' Roll Circus* parties for the Gareth Ivory Foundation. He has also variously worked and played as a reporter, web developer, glockenspiel prodigy and drummer – currently pounding skins for Sydney garage outfit Shakin' Howls.

NICK DENT   JOANNA BOUNDS   DENBY WELLER   DANIEL BISHTON

BEN STUBBS

Ben's job as a travel writer has taken him all the way from camel-wrestling tournaments in Turkey to horseback riding in western Mongolia. When he does make it back to Australia, he calls the northern beaches of Sydney home. He loves the fact that if you do a little digging, the most unusual and authentic travel experiences can be found within easy reach of the L90 bus route he frequently travels.

MELINDA OLIVER

Originally from Melbourne, Melinda thought a year and a half spent in chilly London made moving to sunny Sydney too hard to resist. Sydney's amazing harbour, character-filled suburbs and wildlife (of both the non-human and human variety) sealed the deal. A fashion and features writer, she gets endless inspiration for stories from Sydney's vibrant culture and her spare time is filled with yoga classes and browsing bookstores.

ANNA WARWICK

Anna is a Sydney girl, very much devoted to her beachside home of Bondi. She argues that little compares to a morning swim or surf, a flawless latte in a beachside cafe full of funky peeps, and the plethora of outdoor fun and indoor glamour to be enjoyed day and night. Sydney is far too good to leave, and Anna rarely does, except to quench her endless thirst for worldwide adventure travel.

VALERIE KABOV

Valerie has been a denizen of Sydney's inner-city arts and culture scene for over a decade. Her many sins include running a speakeasy jazz club in Chippendale, knowing the brand of the coffee machine in every cafe within a kilometre radius of the Coca-Cola sign that reigns over the Kings Cross intersection, and publishing a monthly e-newsletter on the state of contemporary and emerging art in Australia.

BEN STUBBS   MELINDA OLIVER   ANNA WARWICK   VALERIE KABOV

hit the streets

> HIT THE STREETS

SYDNEY TRAPEZE SCHOOL

SO YOU THINK YOU CAN FLY

Your toes dangle over the edge of the platform. Your heart thumps beneath your ribs as you hold the bar and jump. Trust me, this is the real thing. The first time you leap off the ledge at the Sydney Trapeze School (STS) is a one-off experience you won't forget in a hurry.

If you ever wanted to join the circus when you were a kid, this is the place to revive your high-flying fantasies. The talented Taylor twins, Frank and Robert, who started the STS, have more than 10 years of international experience in the US, Austria, Singapore, New Caledonia and Thailand between them, so you can feel pretty damn confident about enrolling in a class. Any number of high-wire activities are on offer, including cloud swing (a combination of static and swinging trapeze skills), swinging trapeze, silks and tissue (an aerial 'dance' featuring, would you believe, silks and tissue!) and the heart-stoppingly exciting flying trapeze classes, where you'll finish your instruction being caught mid-flight by the 'catcher' 8 m above the ground!

The STS lives in a warehouse in St Peters within walking distance of the train station, and is the only indoor, all-weather trapeze centre in the city. It's open to the public every day of the week bar Monday, and a single class will set you back $60. They also offer three-for-the-price-of-two lessons and an intensive 10-week course, where you can hone your technique and your physique in preparation for an acrobatic performance in front of an audience of your high-flying peers.

So, the next time you're looking for an unusual way to work up a sweat, head to the STS, chalk up your hands and take flight.

BEN STUBBS

> HIT THE STREETS

1–7 Unwins Bridge Rd, St Peters
(02) 9557 9668
www.sydneytrapezeschool.com.au
Open Tues–Thurs 8am–9pm,
Fri–Sat 8am–10pm, Sun 8am–4pm

See also
map 2 B4

> HIT THE STREETS

THE OLD FITZROY HOTEL

THEATRICAL PUB GRUB

If you think the cost of a night out at the theatre is steeper than Mount Everest, think again. At The Old Fitzroy Hotel you can get their famous 'beer, laksa and a show' ticket for only $35. And on 'cheap Tuesdays' you can get the same amazing deal for a miniscule $25.

The Old Fitz is a cosy timber-and-brick pub with a roaring fire (in winter) and over a dozen beers to choose from. It's perfect for a taste of the 'Old Country' and just what you'd expect from a turn-of-the-century pub. Out the back, the delicious aromas from the wildly popular kitchen fill the air. The aforementioned and justifiably famous laksa comes in gargantuan bowls and is packed with 'expensive' ingredients – prawns, chicken and tofu galore.

Up the narrow staircase, you'll find a chilled-out lounge featuring a never-lonely pool table and the kind of retro decor that improves as the night goes on. It's a different world up here. The urban tunes are more noticeable, the crowd is younger and the vibe is ultra-relaxed.

The jangling of the theatre bell announces that tonight's show is about to begin. Wind your way into the bowels of the pub to the compact theatre with its chipped black walls and friendly bench seating. Home to local legends the Tamarama Rock Surfers' Theatre Company, this playhouse is known for nurturing the rising young stars of independent theatre. You might catch a full-length drama, a spot of hip-hop theatre*, a classic play or a monologue. Whatever's on offer, a high standard is guaranteed.

After the show, hit the bar for a chance to meet the stars or just some of the locals. From diehard theatre-goers and tattooed teens to polite ladies in pearls, this eccentric little venue draws a fantastic crowd.

DENBY WELLER

> HIT THE STREETS

129 Dowling St, Woolloomooloo
(02) 9356 3848
www.oldfitzroy.com.au
www.rocksurfers.org
Pub open Mon–Fri 11am–12am,
Sat 12pm–12am, Sun 3–10pm;
Bistro open Mon–Fri 12–3pm
& 6–9.30pm, Sat–Sun 5–9.30pm;
Stage shows on Tues–Sat 8pm &
Sun 5pm

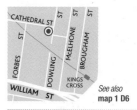

See also
map 1 D6

'ENCYCLO' TRIVIA

* Hip-hop theatre incorporates elements and themes associated with hip-hop music, including breakdancing and rapping, and stories related to the struggles of the hip-hop generation.

> HIT THE STREETS

CLOVELLY BOWLING CLUB

MEMBERS

010

CLOVELLY BOWLING CLUB

BOWL ME OVER

Lawn bowls is a cult pastime in Sydney. But while the older set might still wear whites and bowling shoes, the younger generation has eschewed the rules and regulations, and replaced them with beers and boardies*.

At Clovelly Bowling Club the vibe is decidedly casual. While the club won't actually let you wander barefoot on the greens (like you can at Sydney's 'barefoot' bowling clubs), you can get away with your favourite pair of flip-flops and a smile. A game of bowls plus use of the barbecue is just $10 per person (BYO meat and snags*). The drinks are bloody cheap too. Probably why this venue is so popular with the 'recovery' crowd as well as pretty much everyone else.

The club has an incredible 180-degree ocean vista, so there are plenty of photo opportunities to be had while you're 'putting another prawn on the barbie'. Peer to the left and you can almost spy the supermodels sunbaking at Bondi Beach. To the right, on a clear day, are the towering cliffs of Royal National Park.

Some people might prefer to go to a posh bar in Bondi for their sea views, but you can head to Clovelly Bowling Club for a cut-price version of the same thing, served up with a slice of lime. **JOANNA BOUNDS**

> HIT THE STREETS

Cnr Boundary & Ocean sts, Clovelly
(02) 9665 1507
www.clovellybowlingclub.com.au
Bowls available Mon–Sun 12.30pm
till sunset

See also
map 3 A4

'ENCYCLO' TRIVIA

* 'Boardies' is an Australian slang term for board shorts, the swimming shorts preferred by most male beach-goers around the country, and often worn as regular shorts during summer.

* 'Snags' is an Australian slang term for sausages.

MU-MESON ARCHIVES

CULT CINEMA'S LAST OUTPOST

In the age of YouTube, DVDs and movie downloads, the days of repertory cinema – cheap movie houses showing classic and cult films – would seem to be over. But there is still one place in Sydney screening underground movies and documentaries in a laidback environment encouraging discussion and audience interaction.

The Mu-Meson* Archives is a 40-seater screening room above a furniture warehouse. It's run by Jaimie and Aspasia Leonarder – aka Jay Katz and Miss Death – Sydney counterculture figures renowned for their 'Sounds of Seduction' dance parties in the 1990s. Rabid collectors of old movies on 16 mm and VHS, they show highlights of their collection together with films borrowed from around the world. 'We screen everything that sits outside the margins of mainstream', says Jaimie (an erstwhile host of the SBS channel's *The Movie Show*).

In any given month Mu-Meson Archives might show a forgotten, low-budget horror movie from the 1970s; a 1960s trip-out feature; episodes of the German version of *Star Trek*; or documentaries on subjects such as the occult, Obama's hidden agenda or Seattle grunge. Laughably bad films starring 1980s pop stars are especially popular.

The Leonarders look on their thrice-weekly screenings as community events – just $10 covers the screening, as well as home-cooked soup or cake, and tea or coffee. Their theatrette is crammed with chairs, sofas and film canisters, as well as strange props and totem poles left over from their party nights. Bizarre, bohemian and unlike any cinema you've ever attended, Mu-Meson Archives puts the sheer astonishment back into movie-going.

NICK DENT

> ## > HIT THE STREETS

Cnr Parramatta Rd & Trafalgar St, Annandale
(02) 9517 2010
www.mumeson.org
Open 7.30pm–late on selected weeknights (check program online)

See also
map 2 B1

'ENCYCLO' TRIVIA

* 'Mu' is the name of a mythical, pre-Atlantean civilisation. 'Meson' is Spanish for inn or a place of hospitality. So the name is an apt one for an underground film club screening movies that most people don't know exist.

> **HIT THE STREETS**

CONSERVATION VOLUNTEERS AUSTRALIA

OFF THE BEATEN TRACK

Ever wondered what it would be like to be an eco warrior? Sign up to be a volunteer with Conservation Volunteers Australia and you can experience the natural beauty of Sydney Harbour, and make a difference to the environment at the same time.

As a Conservation Volunteer (CV) for the Sydney Harbour National Park project you get five days' accommodation, food and activities for only $208. In the company of eight like-minded others, CVs get to sleep in comfortable, dorm-style accommodation in the historic refurbished officers' quarters on Middle Head. Your meals will be prepared 'Big Brother style' in the well-equipped kitchen and eaten in the fantastic living quarters with harbour views. After a leisurely 8am start (this is no boot camp!), and under the direction of your team leader, you'll learn the basic skills of bush regeneration, including how to identify noxious weeds and other unwanted introduced species, and replant native vegetation.

Each day you'll get to work at a different location and one of the five days is spent on picturesque Clark or Shark islands. If you're lucky you might see water dragons sunning themselves on the rock shelves around Bradleys Head, bent-wing bats hanging out in the caves at Middle Head or long-nosed bandicoots doing their thing around the barracks at night. Due to the strictly no-alcohol policy, you'll most probably spend your evening 'free time' playing games, going on guided walks, reading and chatting with your fellow CVs. In other words, good clean fun.

As special permits are required for some of the stunning locations you'll be working at, you'll also get to see parts of Sydney Harbour National Park that most locals and tourists never do. Now how's that for feel-good factor? **BEN STUBBS**

> HIT THE STREETS

(02) 9564 1244
www.conservationvolunteers.com.au
Go to 'Conservation Connect' and select Sydney and then the month in which you wish to volunteer for a full list of activities and projects.

See also
map 1 C1

CAMPING ON COCKATOO ISLAND

TENT WITH A VIEW

Sydney is all about harbour views – real estate prices shoot up as soon as you can see an inch of water from your toilet window, and tourists pay dearly for the privilege of waking up to a sparkling vista. But finally there's a cheap place to stay in Sydney that still has unbeatable views of the harbour.

So, roll up your sleeping bag, pack your dinner, and take a 10 min ferry ride from Circular Quay to historic, heritage-listed Cockatoo Island for a camping experience that will make you tweet*. There are 135 camping spots (sans power), and if you don't have your own tent you can hire one. The facilities are excellent: large cooking areas, clean bathrooms with solar-powered showers and a cafe with steaming hot coffee and yummy snacks.

Over the years Cockatoo Island has been home to many things (including a 'reform' school for naughty girls), so once you've pitched your tent, get walking and exploring. Rusty cranes dotted around the island reflect its shipbuilding past. And those holes in the walls of the old convict buildings? So the guards could shoot down prisoners who tried to escape! Check out the Dogleg Tunnel, where a soundscape depicts the 1942 Japanese midget submarine attack on vessels anchored in Sydney Harbour. Free regular art exhibitions add a dash of contemporary culture to the experience.

If none of this interests you, then the water traffic around the island is endlessly entertaining. Ferries and dinghies jostle with luxury boats, while their owners briefly moor to grab takeaway lattes. But at nightfall the quiet island may feel a little eerie, so get comfy in your tent while the sparkling lights of Sydney emerge. And, if you're up early enough, watch the sunrise over the Sydney Harbour Bridge. Cameras essential!

MELINDA OLIVER

> **HIT THE STREETS**

(02) 8898 9774
www.cockatooisland.gov.au
Information centre open
Mon–Sun 9am–5pm

See also
map 1 C3

'ENCYCLO' TRIVIA

* In case you've been hiding under a rock for the past year or so, people who 'tweet' are users of the popular online social networking program, Twitter.

> HIT THE STREETS

SURFING IN MAROUBRA

LEAVE YOUR FEAR AT HOME

According to Maroubra surfing instructor Wigsy, Bondi waves are 'soft and fluffy' compared to the barrels at Maroubra Beach. Located in Sydney's south, Maroubra is renowned for its surfing scene, along with being home to the infamous Bra Boys* gang, who rule the ocean and the streets in this sun-kissed suburb. It adds extra frisson when learning to surf in Maroubra knowing that the Bra Boys will be out in the waves at the north end of the beach, while you'll be safely learning the sport with Sydney Safe Surf School at the more sedate south end.

On arrival, you'll be decked out in the appropriate gear and allocated an 8 ft softboard, which will go easy on your head if you wipe out in the surf (trust me, it's all part of the fun). You'll learn about rips, how to stretch on the beach so you look like a pro and where the beginners' patch of surf is (stay well clear of Bra Boys' territory until you've lost your L plates).

During your first 2 hr lesson ($55 per lesson, or $210 for a course of five) you'll swallow more salt water than you thought was humanly possible, use muscles you didn't know existed and end up with a loose, tingly feeling from the thrill and exertion of it all.

Maroubra is one of only two beaches in Australia to be a dedicated National Surfing Reserve (the other is Bells Beach in Victoria). Learn to surf here and you'll be good enough to take on waves anywhere in the world. Well almost!

JOANNA BOUNDS

> HIT THE STREETS

Sydney Safe Surf School
Maroubra Beach, Maroubra
(02) 9365 4370
www.safesurfschools.com.au
Classes take place every day all
year-round (contact for class times)

Maroubra Beach

See also
map 3 A3

'ENCYCLO' TRIVIA

* The Bra Boys were the subject of a controversial documentary *Bra Boys: Blood is Thicker than Water* (2007), which detailed the gang's history of violent clashes with members of the public and the police from the gang's point of view. The documentary was directed by Sunny Abberton, brother of the gang's founder, Koby Abberton. Actor Russell Crowe provided the narration.

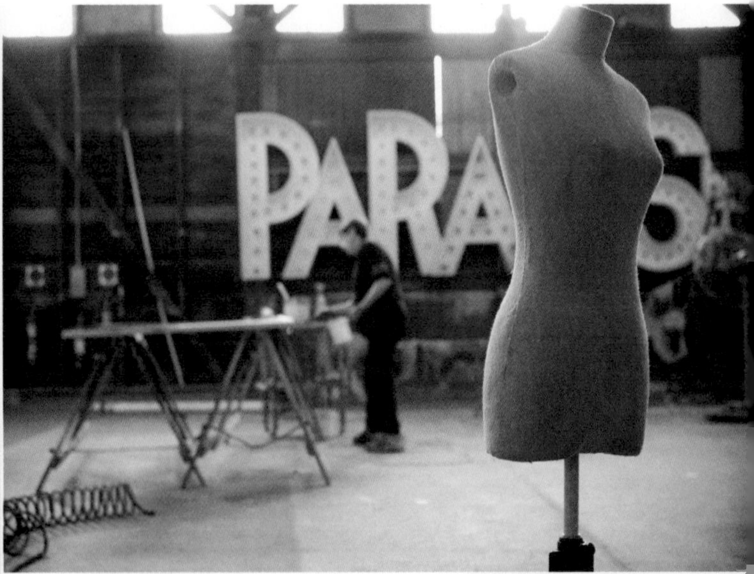
PARA

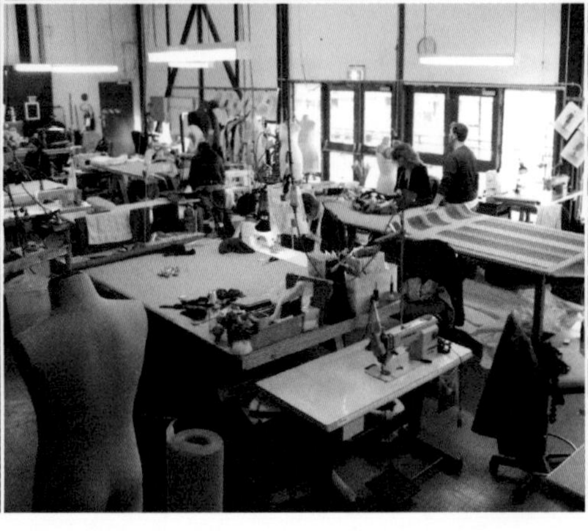

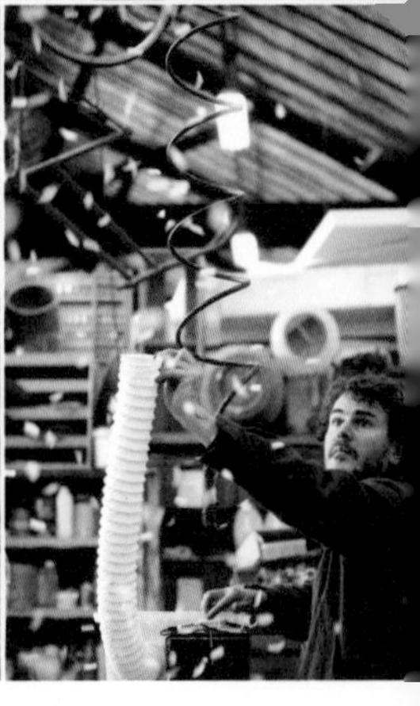

SYDNEY THEATRE COMPANY BACKSTAGE TOURS

THE SHOW MUST GO ON

If you think that seeing behind the scenes of a theatre company might 'ruin the magic', think again. The Sydney Theatre Company (STC), scenically located at The Wharf in Walsh Bay, is one of Australia's top cultural institutions, and its backstage tours at $8 a pop are popular with aspiring young actors and theatre devotees alike.

You'll gather outside the STC box office before heading to historic Wharf 4, where 'the magic' happens. There you'll see how the amazing sets are put together, learn all about those fake, bloodied body parts and other stage trickery in the props department, swoon at the endless racks of shoes and dresses in the costume room, and let out your inner thespian in the rehearsal rooms.

You'll then scoot back to the entrance via the fire tunnel and cross over the road to the main event – The Sydney Theatre – where the tour continues through to the stars' dressing rooms. The STC has helped foster the careers of many top Australian actors, including Cate Blanchett, Toni Collette and Geoffrey Rush, so you never know who you might bump into (no promises, though). You'll then be able to tread the boards of the stage like a pro, check out the complex lighting system and take a seat in the theatre while you fire questions at your expert guide.

By the time you've finished this tour, you'll know for sure that as the curtains come down at the end of another one of STC's brilliant productions, it's the crew as much as the actors who deserve a standing ovation. **MELINDA OLIVER**

> **HIT THE STREETS**

Pier 4, Hickson Rd, Walsh Bay
(02) 9250 1777
www.sydneytheatre.com.au
Tours are held on the 1st and 3rd Thurs
of every month at 10.30am

See also
map 1 B1

CARRIAGEWORKS

GET CARRIED AWAY

Back when a hard day's work meant soot, steam and sweat, the amazing space that is CarriageWorks was home to the Eveleigh Rail Yards. Today, this cleverly renovated, heritage-listed building with its mix of exposed rail tracks, steel beams, original brickwork, machinery, high ceilings and arched windows is a brilliant setting for Sydney's most innovative and interactive contemporary arts space.

But it is not just the building that makes CarriageWorks rock. The place is a thriving hub for resident arts organisations, where creative energy pumps through the building's chic minimalist theatres and galleries on a nightly basis. A huge schedule of events means there is something to suit all tastes, with many for free. Dance, experimental theatre, physical theatre, art exhibitions, installations and film nights are all in the mix. Big name companies perform alongside emerging groups. And, for those seeking something more dynamic, you can get grooving at hip-hop festivals, hit the concrete at break dance classes, or learn the moves from iconic dance films before twisting the night away.

CarriageWorks' huge foyer is regularly used for craft markets (check the website for dates), where you can buy one-off pieces from talented Australian jewellery and fashion designers. On Saturdays, get your fresh Aussie produce at the Eveleigh Farmers' Market opposite the entrance. Hang about for coffee at the über-stylish cafe or mingle in the evening for a drink at the bar before a show.

The great thing about CarriageWorks is that it's not just for folks dressed in black. Its doors are open to anyone who wants to be inspired, challenged or simply entertained. More good reasons to hop on board the next fast train to CarriageWorks. **MELINDA OLIVER**

> ## HIT THE STREETS

245 Wilson St, Eveleigh
(02) 8571 9099
www.carriageworks.com.au
Open Mon–Fri 9am–5pm, Sat 9am–1am
Open evenings for performances

See also
map 2 D2

SYDNEY HARBOUR KAYAKS

PICK UP A PADDLE

Sydney's nightlife can take a toll on your body and after a few bad hangovers, you might be ready to experience another side of the city. Apart from being great exercise, kayaking around Sydney Harbour is one of the best ways to experience the isolated bushland and pristine coves that are as much a part of Sydney as the buskers around Circular Quay.

Head out to The Spit Bridge north of Sydney's CBD where you can sign up for a 4 hr eco tour with Sydney Harbour Kayaks including guides and all your gear for only $99. The eco tour takes in the history of Middle Harbour and Garigal* National Park and finishes off with a beer at the Middle Harbour yacht club (well, you don't want to miss out entirely).

If caffeine is your preferred fix, then the early morning Balmoral coffee tour might be the way to go. The 2.5 hr tour will take you past multi-million dollar yachts and rich folks' mansions into the natural beauty of Middle Harbour. Along the way your clued-up guide will pick a secluded beach and brew a pot of steaming hot coffee for you and your companions, before an appetite-stimulating power paddle back to base.

For those who prefer to go solo, Sydney Harbour Kayaks also rents a range of single and double kayaks. Beginners can also take advantage of kayak lessons when you can learn everything from safety skills to navigation and preparation techniques to ensure you're well equipped for your next kayaking adventure. With over 240 km of shoreline, the whole of Sydney Harbour is the most stunning outdoor 'gym' around, and you'll be sure to look hot for your next night out on the town. **BEN STUBBS**

> HIT THE STREETS

The Spit Bridge, Mosman
(02) 9960 4389
www.sydneyharbourkayaks.com.au
Open June–Aug Wed–Fri 9am–5pm,
Sat–Sun 7.30am–5pm; Sept–May
Mon–Fri 9am–5pm, Sat–Sun 7.30am–5pm

See also
map 1 C1

'ENCYCLO' TRIVIA

* Garigal is a clan name of the Ku-ring-gai Aboriginal people, the original inhabitants of this area.

treasure trove

DOUBLE HAPPINESS FOR SINOPHILES

How would Chairman Mao feel about today's China – still communist, yet beating the West at its own capitalist game? Probably the same way he'd feel about Mao & More, a shop that sells iconography of the People's Republic to decadent Sydneysiders as curios and furnishings. Yes, effigies of Mao are everywhere in this 1000 m2 showroom, just as they were in China during his reign: on heroic propaganda posters surrounded by adoring children; on porcelain figurines; on badges, bags, mugs and even clocks. Practically a museum of communist history, this is where you can also get Chinese magazines from the 1970s, Communist party hats and uniforms, a *Little Red Book** or a big framed poster of smiling factory workers.

But it's not all about the cult of Mao. Another much-loved guy, Buddha, has a strong presence in busts and wooden statues. And naturally there are more red lanterns on display here than in a Chinese New Year parade. They hang from the ceiling in their dozens, together with lucky-charm banners and traditional birdcages (a design flourish, incidentally, that's currently popular in Sydney bars). Rustic Chinese furniture also abounds with the likes of screens, chairs and hand-painted cabinets. An 80-year-old Shaanxi* cabinet in elm, for instance, will set you back $1480, but a charming wooden box might only be $200.

There are cheaper objects too, such as prints of glamorous Shanghai women, fans, decorative porcelain, glassware goldfish and old-fashioned toys. Mao & More is a hard place to beat as a source of affordable, unusual gifts, or for that authentic Asian piece to jazz up your home environment. Hell, you may just start a cultural revolution in your own living room.

NICK DENT

> TREASURE TROVE

267–271 Cleveland St, Surry Hills
(02) 9699 2700
www.maondmore.com
Open Mon–Fri 10am–6pm,
Sat 10am–6pm, Sun 11am–6pm

See also
map 1 A10

'ENCYCLO' TRIVIA

* Mao Zedong's book of quotations is the most printed book in history apart from the Bible. Around six billion copies of the *Little Red Book* were published from 1964 till his death in 1976.

* Shaanxi is a province in northwest China. Its capital is the city of Xi'an, which houses the famous army of terracotta warriors.

FOOTAGE

FOOTWEAR FOR THE FAITHFUL

Footage is a tiny store, tucked below the trendy Surry Hills end of Oxford Street. Step down into the cave-like white space and you'll find a Kubrik-esque* geometrical display dominated by the sneaker, but also featuring jeans, T-shirts, hats and accessories for men, as well as a cute basic women's range. Think timeless cool with an individual twist, but without the designer price tag.

On a Saturday morning, Footage pumps with funky tunes and savvy clientele. Gay and straight couples rub elbows with smart young professionals looking for that classic piece that will set them apart from the (sub)urban crowd.

The genius of this store is the exclusive, international range. Unusual styles from classic brands are personally sourced and directly imported by the store's owners. Basic black, white, grey and navy colourways are consistently delivered across the range. But, if you're after some colour, you'll find a few standout golds, reds and browns among the adidas old-school two-tones, Converse All Stars, Vans, Le Coq Sportif sneakers, ALIFE runners and Nike Airs.

That elusive item – the great men's T – also abounds at Footage. Jeans include 7 for All Mankind, Citizens of Humanity, Earnest Sewn, Paige Premium Denim and Maiden Noir. Jackets from Brent Wilson, Fred Perry or Huffer add some polish. Complete the look with collector's item baseball hats, classic digital watches and eyewear.

Hotfoot it to Footage and you'll find you want to ditch your old wardrobe and spend up large. Gear this good doesn't date in a hurry. So, as the great sneaker prophet says … just do it! `ANNA WARWICK`

> TREASURE TROVE

13C Burton St, Darlinghurst
(02) 9332 1337
www.footage.com.au
Open Mon–Wed & Fri 11am–7pm,
Thurs 11am–8pm, Sat 11am–6pm,
Sun 12–5pm

See also
map 1 C7

'ENCYCLO' TRIVIA

* Stanley Kubrick is widely acknowledged as one of the most innovative, influential and intriguing directors in the history of cinema. This reference is to Kubrick's film *2001: A Space Odyssey* (1968).

> TREASURE TROVE

TITLE

CULTURE HQ

When a visiting French musician says, 'I wish we had a place like this in Paris' about a Sydney store, you know you're on to a really good thing. Hidden in a sleepy part of Crown Street, Surry Hills, between a laundrette and a hairdresser, Title is one of Sydney's very few underground 'destination' shops.

Title's window display makes it almost impossible for anyone interested in 20th-century film, art or music, or just fascinated by 'the path less travelled', to resist walking inside. Godard* and Antonioni* DVD collections sit next to books on contemporary African architecture and selections of the best old-school funk CDs.

If you want an education or a recommendation, talk to Jonathan or James, both of whom are walking, talking music and film encyclopaedias. Try testing them with your curliest request about that late 1980s German band, or the last album by that odd Russian duo and then try to keep your jaw in place as they come up with answers! But don't be surprised to discover that 3 hrs have passed since you walked into Title, after what you thought were just a short 15 min.

You might walk out with an early Queen Latifa vinyl, a Tarkovsky* film, a subversive T-shirt or far more insight into the origins of Mariachi music than you ever thought possible. But, whatever's the case, you will have just found one of the best ways to spend an afternoon in Sydney, with or without a French date.

VALERIE KABOV

> TREASURE TROVE

499 Crown St, Surry Hills
www.titlespace.com
(02) 9699 5222
Open Mon–Wed 10am–6pm,
Thurs 10am–8pm, Fri–Sat 10am–6pm,
Sun 12–5pm

See also
map 1 B9

'ENCYCLO' TRIVIA

* Jean-Luc Godard is a French filmmaker who was a pioneer of French New Wave cinema in the late-1950s and 60s.

* Michelangelo Antonioni was an Italian director who died on the same day as fellow director Ingmar Bergman in 2007. He is best remembered for his film *Blowup* (1966).

* Andrei Tarkovsky was a Russian director best known for his two memorable sci-fi masterpieces, *Solaris* (1972) and *Stalker* (1979).

> TREASURE TROVE

GALLERY SERPENTINE

NAUGHTY BUT NICE

Specialising in corsetry and 'Gothic wear', this sexy little store on Newtown's fringe is a delicious blend of shopping and spectacle, tailor-made for those in search of a walk on the wild side.

Seductive and saucy, Gallery Serpentine's designs run from spicy corsets with names like Spanish Harlot and Femme Fatale, to a fantasy-inducing selection of Victorian-inspired frockcoats and gowns. After something a bit more demure? Then check out the fancy black-on-black lacy shirts and shrugs, or the silhouette-friendly boleros. Or go for the *Nurse Betty** shirt-dress that comes in black (or red) and features PVC cuffs and collars. This is gear with an edge, which you can still take for a spin on the streets of any city without raising an eyebrow.

For fearless fellows there are coats straight out of *The Matrix*, pirate shirts to shame Seinfeld* and bondage kilts with PVC trimmings. And, if you're still thinking Gallery Serpentine is just for women, don't forget everyone looks good in a skull!

The staff at Gallery Serpentine are always happy to lace you into the newest design, and the French boudoir-style change rooms make it easy to act bolder than you may feel. In this velvety wonderland, life as a Goth seems so right. Bat-and-spider-shaped jewellery will suddenly appeal, lace bloomers will beg for attention and fishnet stockings will seem to leap into your hands. Perhaps you'll depart this underworld of Gothic glamour armed with a whole new style, or perhaps you'll sneak away with just a pair of PVC gloves tucked into your handbag. `DENBY WELLER`

> **TREASURE TROVE**

Shop 2, 112–116 Enmore Rd, Enmore
(02) 9557 5821
www.galleryserpentine.com
Open Mon–Wed & Fri 10am–6pm,
Thurs 10am–8pm, Sat 10.30am–5.30pm,
Sun 12–5pm

See also
map 2 B3

'ENCYCLO' TRIVIA

* *Nurse Betty* (2000) is an American black comedy starring Renee Zellweger as a screw-ball, soap opera–loving waitress. For her performance, Zellweger won a Golden Globe Award.

* The pirate shirt appeared in the 'Puffy Shirt' episode of US sitcom *Seinfeld* in 1993. Jerry (Seinfeld) is tricked into wearing the shirt during an appearance on *The Today Show*, and he famously exclaims, 'But I don't want to be a pirate!'.

CYRILS
DAILY SPECIALS
SMOKED SALMON $5.00 250g
BEST COFFEE 250g 3.50
PORT-SALUT CHEESE 2.50
DANISH CAMEMBERT 2.50
REAL-PATÉ TASTY 1.99
SWISS-STYLE CHEESE 7.50 500g
BABYBEL-CHEDDAR 2.50 SPECIAL

THE ART OF FOOD

If you suddenly find yourself craving Polish salami, while looking at video performance art from China, you must be in Hay Street, Chinatown, standing outside **Cyril's Fine Foods** and Gallery 4a.

Everything about Cyril's (starting with the man Cyril himself) is not of this time and place. Don't try to find Cyril's website, he doesn't have one. What he does have is a white coat like a 'proper' delicatessen professional should, loyal assistants who have been with him for decades, a dazzling array of pickled herrings, salami, caviar, conserves, preserves, Riga Sprats*, Suchard Belgian chocolates, Swiss waffles, Dutch crackers and a devilishly addictive Macedonian pepper relish. Cyril has been in the deli business since 1975, and his passion has inspired the kind of customer loyalty that allows his Polish oasis to thrive in the middle of Chinatown.

Unlike Cyril's, **Gallery 4a** (the four 'a's are Australian Asian Art Association) is a relative newcomer to the block. Nestled between a Korean restaurant and a Japanese novelty and clothing store, its white-walled austerity is in stark contrast to the hustle and bustle of Hay Street commerce that buzzes outside the door. Showcasing works and collaborating on exhibitions with artists from across the vast Asian continent, 4a, as befits a 'youngster', is deeply respectful and mindful of its place in Chinatown. The gallery regularly holds public events to involve broader audiences in its work and organises artist-led walking tours of the neighbourhood.

So, whether you're the kind to put the words 'love' and 'herring' in the same sentence, or if you enjoy a serve of culture from anywhere from Iran to Vietnam, Hay Street is a slice of multicultural Sydney that satisfies in every way. VALERIE KABOV

> **TREASURE TROVE**

CYRIL'S FINE FOODS
181 Hay St, Sydney
(02) 9211 0994
Open Mon–Sat 10am–5pm

GALLERY 4A
181–187 Hay St, Sydney
www.4a.com.au
(02) 9212 0380
Open Tues–Sat 11am–6pm

See also
map 1 A7

'ENCYCLO' TRIVIA

* Riga Sprats are a small fish, similar to a sardine, smoked and served in oil. They are a unique delicacy popular in Europe.

BIRD TEXTILES EMPORIUM

PRESERVATION BEFORE PROFITS

Climate-neutral, carbon offsetting and sustainability are buzz words of the noughties, but Bird Textiles Emporium is out to make them last. A sanctuary for funky fabrics, fashions, homewares and gifts, this shop can proudly lay claim to being Australia's first climate-netural business.

Everything about 'Bird' embraces an eco-friendly ethos. All fabrics, created by owner Rachel Bending are hand-printed using water-based dyes on certified organic cotton in her design studio in Byron Bay. Other designs are produced with solar power and to top it off, the company offsets any fuel use.

Even the store fit-out is all about preservation. It lives in a heritage-listed corner building, which was once an 1800s pharmacy. Step inside and you'll find the original glass cabinets, miniature medicine drawers and dark wood display shelves remain, now livened up with Bird Textiles' fresh, colourful products.

New 'guilt-free' print designs are created each season, inspired by nature, Scandinavian and Japanese designs, and 1950s styles. Rachel usually selects one or two key colours per design, such as vivid red, green, blue or chocolate.

The fabrics are then used in the store's fashion garments that range from striking skirts to coats and bags. Your home can undergo the same treatment with pillows, lampshades and even fabric-covered cuckoo clocks for sale. Little gifts such as fabric-covered journals, cards and oh-so adorable buttons will do the trick for friends.

Prices range from just $3 to about $500, and if (on the very odd occasion) you can't find the perfect item, you can just order your favourite product in a winning fabric, and fly away happy. `MELINDA OLIVER`

> TREASURE TROVE

380 Cleveland St, Surry Hills
(02) 8399 0230
www.birdtextile.com
Open Tues–Fri 10am–6pm,
Sat 10.30am–5.30pm

See also
map 1 B10

BOHEMIAN RHAPSODY

Need a new set of duds*? Dig pawing through collections of vinyl and books, finding an obscure item for the kitchen or seeing some live local music on a Saturday morning? Then head to Glebe Markets. A short bus ride or long stroll from the city, Glebe's Saturday markets host a spectacularly diverse set of rotating stalls that attract a motley crew of punters. You can check out the wares, soak up the atmosphere or just kick back on the grass and watch the free bands.

Clothing forms a major chunk of the goods on display, with local and imported vintage garments well represented, complemented by local designers showcasing their latest creations. Home-crafted jewellery, African drums, contemporary sculpture and eco-friendly products are among other desirables you'll find cheek-by-jowl in the bustling stalls. Massage practitioners are on hand if it all gets a bit much. There's even a dedicated alley of international and organic cuisine stalls if you get peckish.

Reclining on the grass for one of the local live acts, you will likely encounter one of the many colourful regulars – perhaps shaking their hips, perhaps offering you some roasted nuts or a sip of their lassi*. When you've done your dash with bohemia, nip out the gate onto the main strip, Glebe Point Road, where you'll find scores of cute cafes, restaurants and pubs to help you find terra firma* again. If you want to, that is.

DANIEL BISHTON

> TREASURE TROVE

**Glebe Public School,
183 Glebe Point Rd, Glebe
(02) 4237 7499
www.glebemarkets.com.au
Every Sat 10am–4pm**

*See also
map 2 D1*

'ENCYCLO' TRIVIA

* 'Duds', an English slang word first appearing in the 1800s, originally referred to old clothing or tattered garments. Today it simply means clothing.

* Lassis are popular, traditional yoghurt-based drinks originally from the Punjab region of the Indian subcontinent.

* 'Terra firma' is a Latin phrase meaning 'solid earth'. Terra: earth, firma: solid.

> TREASURE TROVE

THE STYLE COUNCIL

Just a stone's throw away from the noise and antics of Oxford Street's clubs and bars, the corner of Goulburn and Crown streets marks the start of a more indie view of life. If the high-street fashionistas own Oxford Street, Paddington (up the hill), this part of town is definitely where alternative style-meisters rule.

The corner's most conspicuous star is **Wheels & Dollbaby**, where you can buy sexy little bra-dresses, tops, coats and accessories that are guaranteed to 'snare a millionaire' (as they claim on their website). A black-and-pink paradise of velvet, lace and polka dots, Wheels & Dollbaby is popular with the likes of Amy Winehouse, Kelly Osborne, Pamela Anderson and Deborah Harry.

A couple of doors down is one of the best vintage and retro clothing stores in Sydney, **Grandma Takes A Trip**. Grandma specialises in designer partywear from yesteryear including high-end frocks, coats, hats and accessories from leading 1960s and 70s designers, sourced from Europe and the US. Perfect if you're on the prowl for an outfit that shouts, 'I'm special!'

Not far away is the rock 'n' roll wonderland of **Route 66**. Here you can experience authentic 'Sydney attitude', as the staff are every bit as rock 'n' roll as the store. At Route 66 you'll be able to find those vintage 501s* you've been searching for, western boots, cowboy shirts and a great range of belt-buckles to top off the look.

Now you know where to go next time you need a style reinvention, party outfit or exercise for your credit card!

VALERIE KABOV

> TREASURE TROVE

WHEELS & DOLLBABY
259 Crown St, Darlinghurst
www.wheelsanddollbaby.com
(02) 9361 3286
Open Mon–Wed 10am–6pm,
Thurs 10am–8pm, Fri–Sat 10am–6pm,
Sun 12–5pm

ROUTE 66
225–257 Crown St, Darlinghusrt
www.route66.com.au
(02) 9331 6686
Open Mon–Sat 10.30am–6pm,
Thurs 10.30am–7pm, Sun 12pm–5pm

GRANDMA TAKES A TRIP
263 Crown St, Surry Hills
(02) 9356 3322
www.grandmatakesatrip.com.au
Open Mon–Sat 10am–6pm,
Thurs 10am–8pm, Sun 12pm–5pm

See also
map 1 C7

ROKIT

PLANET VINTAGE

Most days at Rokit you'll be greeted by vintage goddess Pia, sitting proudly behind the counter with her crimson lipstick and fluttering lashes that could take your eye out. With clothing items that will take you back to the days of Grace Kelly and Elizabeth Taylor, Rokit is a happy haven for true vintage buffs. It's just the place to track down stylish apparel and accessories from the Victorian era through to the 1960s.

Whether you're seriously shopping or just browsing, this little house of treasures has something for everyone. There is rare and precious jewellery for serious collectors (make sure to check out the diamonds, pearls, ivory and tortoise shell), and wow-factor stuff for party-goers. Kitsch cocktail wear and crocodile handbags will have costume designers and stylists drooling, while suitably glam costume jewellery will keep debutantes smiling in their ball gowns. There are also 'real' (non-PC*) fur coats and 1920s beaded tunics for those who just want to strut their stuff.

But, if you're thinking the items at this store are likely to be out of your price range, let me tell you that rare and retro doesn't necessarily mean expensive. Yes, there are diamond-encrusted pieces for around $30 000, but there are also bargain sunnies*, sophisticated hip flasks and glitzy earrings for those looking for more affordable accessories.

You can find Rokit right under the shadow of the Sydney Harbour Bridge in the Rocks. It sits snugly in Metcalfe Arcade on George Street alongside other quirky specialty shops such as The Bead Bar. Hop to it.

BEN STUBBS

> **TREASURE TROVE**

Metcalfe Arcade, 80–84 George St, The Rocks
(02) 9247 1332
www.rokit.com.au
Open Mon–Sun 10am–5.30pm

See also
map 1 B2

'ENCYCLO' TRIVIA

* 'PC' is an acronym for 'politically correct' and is used to refer to popular attitudes or policies. In recent times, fur has become an unfashionable product as people become more aware of animal rights.

* 'Sunnies' is a common Australian abbreviation for sunglasses.

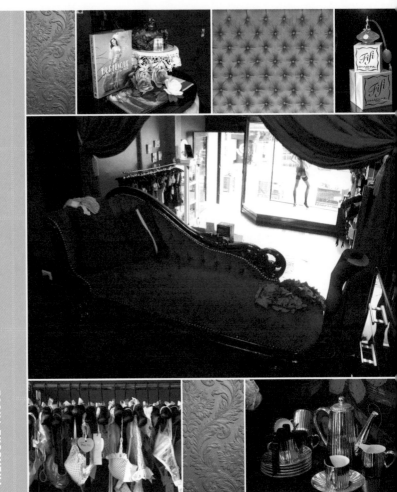

DIRTY PRETTY THINGS

VAVAVOOM!

Even in the bright and bustling intersection that is Paddington's Five Ways, you can't miss the Dirty Pretty Things (DPT) store – there's always a scantily clad mannequin on display in the huge black window. She may be cast as a pin-up Dorothy* in a red-checked frilly ensemble; or as a starlet in silky, pink boudoir attire; or as a saucy madam with a sexy, black lace corset and a feathered mask.

Inside, the store is painted in dramatic blacks and reds, and decked out in luxurious velvet curtains, mirrors, a zebra-print rug and cushioned furnishings. The racks are lined with bras, knickers, corsets and girdles dolled up with bows, lace ribbons, sequins and animal prints. On the cabinet shelves are slippers, teddies, riding crops and garters. These exquisite pieces are sourced from all over the world and among the best upcoming Australian talent.

Pilgrims to DPT get their real kicks in the upstairs viewing room. It's fitted out like a Parisian boudoir with chandeliers and opulent gold dressing rooms, and personal fittings begin with a glass of bubbly on the chaise lounge. If you're a man looking to spoil his leading lady, don't be shy. The DPT team will help you find that perfect something to make your Mrs – or even your mistress – gasp and swoon at your impeccable taste.

More than just a store, DPT is often transformed at night into an art gallery or a salon. The black curtains are drawn, absinthe* cocktails are poured and ladies pay homage to burlesque by learning a strip tease, how to pin and curl their hair, play the ukulele or twirl a hula hoop. Imagine yourself as a Vargas* girl in a 1940s poster – now you're getting the dirty, pretty picture.

ANNA WARWICK

> ## TREASURE TROVE

225 Glenmore Rd, Paddington
(02) 9331 2066
www.dirtyprettythings.com.au
Open Mon, Tues, Wed & Fri 10am–6pm,
Thurs 10am–7pm, Sat 10am–5pm

See also
map 1 E8

'ENCYCLO' TRIVIA

* Dorothy was transported to the magical Land of Oz in the musical-fantasy *The Wizard of Oz* (1939) starring Judy Garland.

* Absinthe: see 'Encyclo' Trivia entry on page 63.

* Alberto Vargas was a noted painter of 1940s pin-up girls and erotica.

feeling peckish?

050

> FEELING PECKISH?

MAMAK

SPICY MALAYSIAN, SINFULLY CHEAP

The queues snaking out onto Goulburn Street tell you everything you need to know about Mamak*, a bustling BYO diner serving authentic Malaysian street food. The intense flavours of Malaysian cuisine are served up here from a concise menu on which nothing costs over $16 and many treats are under $10. Don't be shy to join the line: it moves quickly, and the wait is made all the more entertaining by the storefront spectacle of chefs rolling, twirling and frying roti – crisp flatbread that's fluffy on the inside and ideal for soaking up curry.

Inside the decor is simple but stylish, with wooden tables and stools set against a red-themed interior. And the no-fuss table service means that the main attraction, the food, is soon on its way to you. For a wallet-pleasing entree you can get a plate of plain roti canai with two vegetarian curries and a dollop of hot sambal (a rich chilli paste). It's ideal paired with the best chicken satay sticks in town or a nasi lemak, the Malaysian national dish of coconut rice, peanuts, crisp anchovies, cucumber, hard-boiled egg and feverishly hot sambal. Unmissable mains include kari kambing (a rich curry of slow-cooked lamb) and kari ikan, a tangy fish and okra curry. Cool your mouth with a sweet and milky teh tarik – tea that is 'stretched' or poured from one jug to another until it's a bubbling froth. Finish it all off with ais kacang, a classic Asian dessert of shaved ice, sweetened milk, jelly and red beans, or a roti tisu – a thin, crisp sugar roti rolled into a gravity-defying witch's hat.

Get a group together, order as many different things as you can, and eat your fill for under $25. You'll leave feeling higher than the Petronas Towers*.

`NICK DENT`

> FEELING PECKISH?

15 Goulburn St, Haymarket
(02) 9211 1668
www.mamak.com.au
Open Mon–Sun 11.30am–3pm
& 5.30pm till late

See also
map 1 A7

'ENCYCLO' TRIVIA

* A 'mamak' is a Malaysian stall selling street food. The term originates from the Tamil term for 'uncle'; children patronising the stall would call the shopkeeper 'uncle' as a mark of respect.

* Built in 1998, the Petronas Twin Towers loom over the Malaysian capital Kuala Lumpur. They were the tallest buildings in the world until 2004. Burj Dubai in Dubai, United Arab Emirates, is the tallest man-made structure in the world today.

> FEELING PECKISH?

THE RUM DIARIES

A RUM DO

Reminiscent of a bohemian speakeasy, it's hard to distinguish the staff from the patrons at The Rum Diaries. Everything about this restaurant and bar is a little cheeky, and little wonder given that it draws inspiration from Hunter S. Thompson's* novel, *The Rum Diary**.

Outside The Rum Diaries is painted a mysterious black, but inside the restaurant is an inviting sculptural collage of wooden furniture and quirky decor – the bar and tables are cobbled together from antique mirrors, railway sleepers, school desks and World War II carrying cases. An upright piano sits against one wall and ceiling fans whirr overhead. You could be forgiven for pulling out a Cuban cigar and saying huskily, 'Play it again Sam'*.

In the bright-blue, Barcelona-style tiled kitchen, Fedora-wearing head chef Daniel Brown can be seen visibly enjoying his work. Brown's lauded tapas menu pays tribute to the rum theme in a series of 'Rum Diaries' – innovative food and rum combos. Organic salmon ceviche dressed with Bloody Mary jelly cubes is a house favourite, while Brown's culinary version of tequila, salt and lime is just sublime: take a mouthful of eggplant and gorgonzola tapenade, then sip on an ice-cold rhubarb and berry rum shot, and end with a trio of grapes marinated in Plum Pisco*.

The Diaries' bar is stocked with over 100 rum brands to fix a plethora of fanciful cocktails. A must-try is the Rum Blazer, a spicy drink mixed at your table in a balloon glass then set alight, creating a licking blue flame. If it all gets too much then head to the intimate back room. But don't be surprised when the restaurant manager pops out from behind a bookshelf – it's the secret door to her office!

ANNA WARWICK

> ## > FEELING PECKISH?

288 Bondi Rd, Bondi
(02) 9300 0440
www.therumdiaries.com.au
Open Mon–Sat 6pm–12am,
Sun 6pm–10pm

See also
map 3 B2

'ENCYCLO' TRIVIA

* Hunter S. Thompson was an American journalist and author.

* Set in Puerto Rico in the 1950s, *The Rum Diary* is an upcoming feature film based on Hunter S. Thomson's novel of the same name. Starring Johnny Depp, the film is scheduled for release in 2010.

* 'Play it again Sam' is a famous misquote from the iconic, Academy Award-winning *Casablanca* (1942) starring Humphrey Bogart and Ingrid Bergman. What Bergman actually said was, 'Play it, Sam. Play "As Time Goes By".'

* Plum Pisco is created by macerating fresh plums in Pisco, a South American liquor, distilled from grapes, for six months.

> FEELING PECKISH?

CAFE ISH

BUSH TUCKER TURNS JAPANESE

Sydney is a city obsessed with brunching, yet your average, overpriced cafe rarely serves anything more exciting than bacon and eggs (and smiles from the staff aren't included in the bill). But one tucked-away cafe is serving remarkable things to a clued-in clientele whom the owners take the time to get to know personally.

Cafe Ish is an unassuming 'hole in the wall', a block down the hill from the overcrowded, overrated Crown Street cafe scene. The cafe seats about 20 and the design here is nothing flash – laminex tables and stools inside and out. Banquettes line the narrow indoor area, from which frequent customers sip coffee and trade banter with the kitchen staff. Meet your hosts: chef Josh, a classic Aussie bloke, and barista Ai, from Niigata in Japan. This unlikely couple offers an exciting fusion of organic native ingredients (such as kangaroo, crocodile, wattle and rosella) with Japanese flavours and techniques. And if this sounds unappetising, then you haven't tried the soft-shell crab eggs benedict*.

If you like omelettes, then why not have one Japanese style with pumpkin and minced pork? Wattleseed pancakes come with banana, bacon and maple syrup, or you can try a savoury okonomiyaki – a traditional cabbage pancake with plum barbecue sauce, wasabi mayonnaise, shaved bonito and seaweed. A popular snack is 'Croc in a Rock' – a toad in the hole* using slices of crocodile sausage – and all muffins, scones, cakes and biscuits are baked by Josh on the premises. Ai's coffee is excellent, including lattes sweetened with macadamia syrup and spiced with ground wattleseed.

But don't worry if you do opt for plain bacon and eggs – Cafe Ish has got it covered. NICK DENT

> FEELING PECKISH?

Shop 2, 102 Albion St, Surry Hills
(02) 9281 1688
Open Mon–Fri 7am–4pm, Sat–Sun
8am–2pm (closed long weekends)

See also
map 1 B8

'ENCYCLO' TRIVIA

* Eggs benedict is a breakfast dish of poached eggs on toast with hollandaise sauce, usually served with ham or bacon.

* Traditionally, toad in the hole is an English dish of sausages in Yorkshire pudding batter. Apparently, the dish resembles a toad sticking its head out of a hole.

UCHI LOUNGE

FOR THE SAKE OF SAKE

Uchi Lounge has provided tantalising respite from the chaotic spectacle of nocturnal Oxford Street for the past 12 years. The place is instantly welcoming – upon stepping inside the beautifully renovated terrace, you enter a softly lit bar adorned with original Japanese paintings and boasting a mouth-watering list of Japanese beers, exotic cocktails, and imported and house-made flavoured sakes (ranging from warm, dry umeboshi* to chilled pineapple and clove infusions). Try a Shoga Teenie on for size – Uchi's take on a dry martini with house-made ginger sake, gin and Noilly Prat*. For the lager louts, Uchi's Sake the Bomb dunks a shot of chilli sake into a stein of draft Sapporo beer to memorable effect.

Heading upstairs, you'll find sharp and attentive waiters who genuinely enjoy describing the creative Japanese-Australasian fusion dishes that fill the menu. Chilled wasabi and coriander mussels compete with garlic-and-black-pepper-coated tuna sashimi doused in a leek and sesame soy dressing. And that's just for starters. Wait till you try the baked eggplant in pure miso and Parmesan: it's vegetarian heaven. Sharing is recommended as the portions aren't colossal, but for any missing heft the spectacular presentation and delicately mixed flavours more than compensate. Particularly if you wash everything down with something from the comprehensive list of Japanese vodkas and sakes.

While still a relatively well-kept secret, Uchi Lounge won't take bookings on weekends, and the place starts to pack out with Sydney's fashionably attired 'cool set' from about 7.30pm. No matter though, just order another Shoga Teenie until your table's free. **DANIEL BISHTON**

> **FEELING PECKISH?**

15 Brisbane St, Surry Hills
(02) 9261 3524
www.uchilounge.com.au
Open Mon–Sat 6.30–11pm

See also
map 1 B7

'ENCYCLO' TRIVIA

* Umeboshi is a sour-tasting pickled Japanese fruit, related to a plum or apricot, often served as a side with dinner (prepare your tastebuds!).

* Noilly Prat is a dry vermouth sometimes referred to as 'French vermouth'.

> FEELING PECKISH?

CORELLI'S CAFE GALLERY

LARGE SERVINGS ... OF ATTITUDE

To survive – and thrive – on Newtown's King Street, a cafe must offer something special. Bizarrely named after an 18th-century composer, Corelli's is a Newtown landmark that definitely fits the bill. The servings here are enormous, so whether you hanker for a burrito that could feed a small nation, or a steak sandwich with an inspired fried egg draped across it, the menu is diverse and pleasing. The coffee is also topnotch, and their enormous pot of chai is justifiably famous across all four corners of the globe.

The cafe's diverse crowd makes this one of the best spots in Sydney to indulge in some serious people-watching. On any given day at Corelli's, you may rub shoulders with yuppies, hippies, tattooed types, outlandish performing arts students, theatre-goers from the two nearby theatres, or miscellaneous hungry locals who head to Corelli's for a nosh-up* before they hit one of Newtown's many pubs. The footpath tables are a great place to just 'hang' on sunny afternoons, and at night the cafe's cosy, red-walled interior buzzes with activity. Mod rock, laughter and spirited conversation fill the air while the tiled mosaic portrait of Corelli himself looks on benignly.

If it's simpering, chirpy wait staff you're looking for, go elsewhere. The service at Corelli's is moody, but rather than taking offence most patrons seem to enjoy the challenge. For them, it's all part of the authentic Newtown experience.

DENBY WELLER

> ### > FEELING PECKISH?

352 King St, Newtown
(02) 9550 4080
Open Mon–Sun 7am–12am

See also
map 2 B3

'ENCYCLO' TRIVIA

* 'Nosh-up' is a British slang word for a good meal.

> FEELING PECKISH?

BODHI BAR

BODHILICIOUS!

The advantages of vegan yum cha? It doesn't harm animals or the waistline; it's satisfying and delicious; and it won't leave you in a 'food coma' the way pork buns will. It's this heavenly afterglow, plus a tranquil setting, that make Bodhi Bar a zen oasis in the city.

Despite its central location – a stone's throw from the Domain and and directly across Hyde Park from the CBD – Bodhi Bar can be tricky to find. Check under the plaza beside St Mary's Cathedral. For a hidden restaurant that doesn't advertise, Bodhi Bar does a roaring trade. Rave, word-of-mouth reviews have even reached the ears of travelling celebs like Keanu Reeves, Moby and Ben Lee, so expect the crowds that assemble in the earthy minimalist interior, or outside in the leafy courtyard.

The menu is created almost entirely from fresh, organic fruit and vegetables. Grab the sensational English spinach and tofu dumplings, the tempura field mushrooms, and the mixed pumpkin, snow pea sprout, carrot and ginger dumplings. Bodhi Bar is also famous for its faux-meat dishes. Mr Fan, the head chef, has somehow managed to invent a faux tempura prawn with the exact consistency and texture of seafood, seasoned with a tangy salt, pepper and chilli dressing. The Bodhi Peking 'duck' with a barbecue sauce and mint pancake is also a must-try.

For the evening trade, yum cha items reappear as entrees. Mains include laksa, stir-fries and a green curry with lychee and asparagus. For dessert, try the sour orange sago with mango sorbet or the mango mousse with Frangelico cream and a lychee sago shot. The bar serves cocktails and beer, and you can BYO wine. This is vegan food even hard-core carnivores can get into.

`ANNA WARWICK`

> **FEELING PECKISH?**

**Cook & Phillip Park Leisure Complex,
Cnr College & William sts, Sydney
(02) 9360 2523
Mon 10am–4pm, Tues–Sun 10am–10pm**

*See also
map 1 C6*

DOMA BOHEMIAN BEER CAFE

CZECH IT OUT

A meal at Doma Bohemian Beer Cafe is the kind of experience you'll still be talking about in six months. Although it's a million miles from the cobblestone streets of Prague, it's as close as you'll get to a real Central European dining experience (right down to the whitewashed walls and dark wood furniture) without taking a plane trip.

With a menu that includes a 'steak' of Dutch Edam cheese, a slow-roasted half duck served with sauerkraut and red cabbage, and a mixed platter of roast pork leg, pork schnitzel, smoked pork loin, cheese kransky*, sauerkraut* and dumplings, you'll wish you had three stomachs. The food is not just good; it's heart-stoppingly, mouth-wateringly good – especially if you bring your thirst with you. Featuring famed brews from Belgium, Germany and the Czech Republic, Doma's beer selection is the stuff dreams are made of for Bohemian beer lovers.

For a real taste of Doma start your evening with a mulled wine, then experiment with an absinthe* cocktail and round it all off (if you're still standing) with a glass of grog. Grog is what happens when you take wildly alcoholic Czech rum, add hot water and squeeze in a few drops of lemon. This drink must be why God invented winter!

The crowd at Doma is a movable feast: rowdy and boisterous on weekends (think backpacker reunions), but more subdued on weeknights when you will encounter small groups of diners, family outings and hand-holding couples. If your waiter is anything less than wonderful, you've stumbled into some other restaurant. As the night goes on, and your neighbouring tables are suddenly filled with your new best friends, your every wish will be accommodated – maybe even your desire to meet The Green Fairy*.

DENBY WELLER

> FEELING PECKISH?

29 Orwell St, Potts Point
(02) 9331 0022
www.unasdoma.com.au
Open Mon–Sat 12pm–12am,
Sun 12–10pm

See also
map 1 E6

'ENCYCLO' TRIVIA

* Kransky is a type of meat sausage.

* Sauerkraut is finely shredded cabbage that has been fermented or 'pickled'.

* Absinthe is a highly alcoholic, green-coloured spirit that was popular in 19th century bohemian circles. The original drink, which contained the herb wormwood, is said to have caused visions of a mythical creature named The Green Fairy. However, according to some sources, absinthe's hallucinogenic properties were largely exaggerated.

gertrude & alice

> FEELING PECKISH?

GERTRUDE & ALICE CAFE BOOKSTORE

LITERARY APPEAL

As well as attracting the 'beautiful people', Bondi Beach is home to a large percentage of Sydney's creative types. Artists, writers, photographers, musos and actors all convene at this cosy second-hand bookshop and cafe (the name is a tribute to Gertrude Stein and Alice B. Toklas*) to read, write screenplays, talk shop, brainstorm and catch up. They lounge on couches, perch at tables among the jam-packed bookshelves or dine alfresco on the street.

Chance encounters with friends and strangers are the norm. The result is a lively atmosphere bursting with intellectual and creative energy. The coffee also helps – a sensational blend expertly brewed by the cafe's down-to-earth staff. Meals are fresh, healthy and generous. Recommended are the corn-fritter stack on baby spinach with avocado or bacon, the grilled haloumi* and roast kumara* salad with lentils and greens, and the filling Moroccan lentil stew with yoghurt and bread.

Given that there are over 25 000 titles to entice you, it's almost impossible to leave Gertrude & Alice (G & A) without a volume in hand. Thanks to book expert Jane Turner, who haunts Sydney's garage sales and auctions as well as shipping in books from the US, you may find treasures like a first edition of *The Bell Jar* by Sylvia Plath*, an autobiography of Frank Sinatra signed by the man himself, or a limited edition of *The Last Night on Earth*, signed by Charles Bukowski*.

G & A is the kind of cafe where, whether you come alone or with a friend, you will linger to people-watch, browse or have another soy chai. And, whether you're a professional artiste or a dabbler, you're bound to be hit by a passing flash of inspiration. ANNA WARWICK

> FEELING PECKISH?

46 Hall St, Bondi Beach
(02) 9130 5155
www.gertrudeandalice.com.au
Open Mon–Sun 7.30am–9.30pm

See also map 3 B1

'ENCYCLO' TRIVIA

* Gertrude Stein was an American writer whose Parisian home '27' was a sanctuary for artists like Pablo Picasso. Alice B. Tolkas was Stein's long-time companion and assistant.

* Haloumi is a mild, semi-firm cheese from Cyprus.

* Kumara is also known as sweet potato.

* Sylvia Plath was a 20th-century American poet and author. Gwenyth Paltrow played Plath in *Sylvia* (2003).

* Charles Bukowski was a 20th-century German-American poet, novelist, and short story writer. *The Last Night on Earth* is the last set of poems published during his lifetime.

065

BRAZUCA RESTAURANT & CHURRASCARIA

ALL YOU CAN MEAT

A 30 min ferry ride from Circular Quay, the beachside suburb of Manly is home to a burgeoning South American community. Which is why Brazilian restaurant Brazuca is one of the most buzzing joints in town.

Brazuca's owners, a Manly local and his Brazilian girlfriend, understand it's all about location, location, location. Relax at the beachfront tables, take in the ocean views and sip on a Corona while you wait for your food to arrive. You won't have to stress about what to order here either – the main attraction is a churrascaria, an all-you-can-eat meat barbecue.

Best to arrive early to get the best cuts. For $38 a head, you'll be served small bowls of potato salad, tomato salsa, black beans and 'pao de quiejo' (small warm rolls of Brazilian cheese bread) before the 'meat waiter' arrives at your table with freshly cooked meat or seafood on a spit.

One by one, sirloin steak, chilli mussels, lamb, crispy pork belly, chorizo sausage and chicken in pesto sauce on large skewers are finely shaved at your table and placed on your plate with tongs. The food just keeps coming at Brazuca, so go easy on the first offerings if you want a second serving of your favourite dish. Palate-cleansing cinnamon-spiced pineapple caps off the meal.

The crowd is mostly locals and South American food fans. If you're lucky, you might arrive on the same night as a Brazilian wedding reception; we did, and we all went home with a piece of cake in our pockets. A brilliant venue for birthday bashes and pretty much any group gathering where fun and a big feed are essential, Brazuca serves up a magnificent meat feast to a bossa nova* soundtrack. **JOANNA BOUNDS**

> FEELING PECKISH?

48 North Steyne, Manly
(02) 9977 6307
www.brazucamanly.com.au
Open Mon–Sun 6.30pm–late (dinner),
Sat–Sun 11.30am–4.30pm (lunch)

SYDNEY RD
NTH STEYNE
WEST ESP
EAST ESP
STH STEYNE
Manly Beach
Manly Cove

See also map 1 C1

'ENCYCLO' TRIVIA

* Bossa nova, Portuguese for 'new trend', is a style of Brazilian music. Although the bossa nova movement only lasted six years (1958–63), it contributed a number of songs to the standard jazz repertoire.

> FEELING PECKISH?

GOVINDA'S RESTAURANT AND MOVIE ROOM

KRISHNA LIKED MOVIES TOO

Named after Krishna, the spiritual embodiment of all things fun, Govinda's is a two-in-one experience that's literally consciousness-raising. Just over $28 will get you a dinner-and-movie ticket that will satisfy all five senses in a way that could just possibly get you to nirvana status.

With a balcony overlooking buzzing Darlinghurst Road and an eclectic crowd of diners, the restaurant is a favourite haunt for Gen Xs and Gen Ys from all walks of life. The opulent buffet serves up ultra-wholesome and entirely meat-free pastas, daals and curries. All the dishes are richly flavoured – guaranteed to appeal even to confirmed carnivores – and the all-you-can-eat factor means nobody ever goes hungry. Bookings are essential on weekends and advisable on weeknights. Be sure to arrive at least half an hour before your movie's scheduled screening time, as the queue for the buffet can slow down the dining process a little.

Moving through to the boutique movie room with its carpeted walls, this is where you can check out current Hollywood blockbusters as well as thoughtfully selected independent releases. Govinda's is the only cinema in Sydney where you can kick off your shoes and sprawl on custom-made floor cushioning or sink into a squashy couch. And, as you'd expect of any good cinema, there's a state-of-the-art screen and surround sound. The experience is all so good you'll want to come back again and again. A bit like reincarnation really.

DENBY WELLER

> **FEELING PECKISH?**

112 Darlinghurst Rd, Darlinghurst
(02) 9380 5155
www.govindas.com.au
Restaurant open Mon–Sun 5.45–10pm
Check website for movie program and
session times.

See also
map 1 D7

night owl

> NIGHT OWL

THE HOPETOUN HOTEL

IT'S A LONG WAY TO THE TOP...

Where would Sydney's independent live music scene be without The Hoey? Up a certain creek without a paddle, that's where. Night in, night out, The Hopetoun Hotel's been supporting the small fries before they turn into big spuds for much longer than your average rocker's memory reaches.

At first glance, The Hopetoun appears to be just another well-seasoned, intimate little pub with a smallish stage. But don't be fooled. The Hoey regularly reels in the big fish as well as the small fries, showcasing international indie acts you wouldn't normally expect to see at such a small venue. Most nights, though, The Hoey focuses on doing what it does best, presenting popular independent Australian bands.

The bar staff have a unique, hands-on approach to running The Hoey that makes the place feel like you're watching a gig in your mate's lounge room. With much better sound and a fully stocked bar, of course. The pool table out back, basement full of vintage pinball and arcade machines, and a glorious absence of invasive poker machines all add to The Hoey's homely atmosphere.

Fancy a feed before your slab of rock? Just upstairs is Rider, The Hopetoun's own Mexican restaurant. Rider puts its own spin on fresh and authentic Mexican dishes at dirt-cheap prices. Hint: the garlic and mushroom quesadilla* is a winner. Grab a bottle of red from the bar downstairs and they'll mix you a jug of sangria that'll put hairs on your chest.

If you want to witness Australian independent music live in its natural habitat any night of the week, you owe yourself a trip to The Hopetoun.

DANIEL BISHTON

> **NIGHT OWL**

416 Bourke St, Surry Hills
(02) 9361 5257
www.myspace.com/hopetounhotel
Open Mon–Sun 4.30pm–12am

See also
map 1 C9

'ENCYCLO' TRIVIA

* Quesadilla, literally a 'little cheesy thing', is a Mexican snack food made of cheese wrapped in uncooked masa (cornmeal dough) and fried, or cooked inside a corn, wheat or flour tortilla.

> NIGHT OWL

TIME TO VINO

A TOP DROP IN

In recent years Sydney has embraced the Italian-style wine bar like a mamma embraces her bambino. Time to Vino in Stanley Street, Sydney's original little Italy, was among the first of the town's new wave of 'enotecas' – where punters can sit in comfort, have drinks and pasta brought to them, wear lots of black and say 'ciao' a lot.

The name 'Time to Vino' is a variation on the phrase 'beer o'clock', that is, time to down tools at work and have a refreshing beverage. And, while you can get the amber nectar here, it really is all about the wine. The bar is owned by young sommelier* Clint Hillery, who stocks a great list of European and Antipodean wines that are available by the glass, by the carafe (250 ml), or by the bottle; a typical glass of something excellent costs $10. You don't have to be a wine expert to have a good time here: witty and knowledgeable waiters patrol the two-level bar's wooden high and low tables, ready to give counsel on the perfect drop to suit your mood, or your meal.

Chalked on a blackboard, the ever-changing 'Booze Food' menu is divided into three categories: 'Waiting for Friends' (appetisers to share), 'Friends are Here' (pasta and salad mains) and 'Who Needs Friends' (desserts). Start with some tomato and mozzarella arancini* or a trio of fresh shucked Coffin Bay oysters. Your main might be a rich and hearty lamb ragu with orecchiette* or lemony spaghettini with white anchovies, garlic and cauliflower. Desserts range from house-made lemon tart to 'Adult Sundaes' – gelato spiked with liqueurs such as Pedro Ximénez and Moscato. Bene, bene*.

NICK DENT

> NIGHT OWL

66 Stanley St, East Sydney
(02) 9380 4252
www.timetovino.com
Open Mon–Sat 4pm–late

See also
map 1 C6

'ENCYCLO' TRIVIA

* A sommelier is a wine expert who composes wine menus, maintains a wine cellar and offers advice to customers.

* Arancini literally means 'little oranges'; it refers to crumbed Sicilian rice balls.

* Orecchiette, or 'little ears', are ear-like folds of pasta, native to the Puglia region of Italy. 'Ragu' is meat sauce.

* In Italian, 'bene, bene' literally means 'well, well'. In English it is generally understood to mean 'good, good'.

RUBY RABBIT

ADVENTURES IN CLUBLAND

You'd be forgiven for thinking you'd slipped down a rabbit hole into Alice's wonderland at the blink-now-and-you'll-miss-it Ruby Rabbit club on Oxford Street in Darlinghurst.

The De Nom room is the jewel in the crown of this three-level nightspot. Featuring 23-carat gold gilded wall panelling and cascading chandeliers, it's where international guests like Snoop Dogg, the Foo Fighters and Mick Jagger have indulged in the regal madness (you really must visit the 'throne' toilets) and relaxed opulence that characterises this sparkling venue.

Below De Nom is the Houndstooth room, an intimate space for drinkers with over 100 cocktails to choose from. In the room's corner sits a stylised phone booth that provides fingerprint-scan-only access for VIPs who need their private space. If you're lucky enough to be 'somebody', you'll gain entry to the aptly named Ribald suite, complete with a sunken lounge and spa, and your very own bartender in the cupboard to mix your margaritas.

But don't worry if you're just a happy 'nobody'. You might not gain access to the club's inner sanctums, but you'll still have a great time exploring the all-access areas including the newly completed Big Rig Diner on street level, where you can indulge in a gourmet hot dog and boogie to the 60s and 70s tunes belting out of the jukebox.

Ruby Rabbit offers an attention to detail and a sense of humour not often seen by Sydney night owls. With its three distinctly themed floors, it's the perfect place to celebrate a birthday, hold a wrap party or magazine launch, or just to let your hair down and party into the wee hours with all the other mad hatters. **BEN STUBBS**

> NIGHT OWL

231 Oxford St, Darlinghurst
(02) 9332 3197
www.rubyrabbit.com.au
Open Tues–Sat 9pm till late

*See also
map 1 C8*

CAFE HERNANDEZ

THE 24/7 FIX

Scenario 1: It's 3am, you're on to your fourth nightclub in Kings Cross and your hot date just developed a need for hot chocolate and quiet conversation, while waiting for a second wind to kick in. Scenario 2: It's 11am, you've just dragged yourself out of bed and are badly in need of a seriously strong cup of java. Scenario 3: It's 1am and you're keen to rub shoulders with a diverse crowd, ranging from taxi drivers to some of Sydney's literati, all under the watchful eye of Mona Lisa.

What to do? Head to the legendary Cafe Hernandez – a Sydney institution that has been catering to caffeine addicts and insomniacs for almost four decades. The Hernandez family has been roasting coffee for Sydneysiders way before lattes and cappuccinos became the go, handing down their distinctive traditional roasting and blending techniques from generation to generation.

The cafe's warm, orange glow and cheerful red awning have seduced many a late-night wanderer into this tiny outcrop of old Europe, that's seemingly shipwrecked on the side of the Cross City Tunnel. Every square inch of the cafe is crammed with things useful and curious – and usually both – from the walls decorated with copies of old masterpieces (like the fake Mona Lisa), to the puzzling ancient piano guarding a glorious coffee-roasting drum. The counter display groans with Portuguese tarts, chorizo rolls and tortillas, as well as antique coffee-making appliances. But the main event is the coffee. Beans are sourced from around the world – Brazil, Kenya, Indonesia; you name it, they've got it.

VALERIE KABOV

> NIGHT OWL

60 Kings Cross Rd, Potts Point
(02) 9331 2343
www.cafehernandez.com.au
Open 24 hrs, including all
public holidays

See also
map 1 E7

> NIGHT OWL

SOUND LOUNGE

FOOT TAPPING RECOMMENDED

Breezing past the bright lights of the Seymour Centre, you'd never realise that it conceals a lynchpin of Sydney's contemporary jazz and improvised music scene. Slyly nestled in the centre's basement, Sound Lounge has been the Sydney Improvised Music Association's haunt since 2005, showcasing local, interstate and international talent from Tuesday to Saturday nights.

Chosen for its taut acoustics and generous views of the stage, this intimate 120-seat venue draws a dedicated throng of jazz freaks, from swingin' young things to ageing hipsters. In terms of the sounds on offer, the Sound Lounge mixes up the music genres. Wandering downstairs on any given night, you may find yourself immersed in an alien soundscape of electromechanical experiments, or the smoked-out den of a 50s-style cool jazz trio. The bar's 1am license sweetens the deal, but this place is all about the music – an excited hush descends during sets, broken only by applause for solos, which may be polite or rapturous, depending on the crowd's verdict.

While weekly doses of hot jazz and experimental improvisations are the Sound Lounge's bread and butter, there's a spicy garnish on the first Thursday of each month. The night's aptly named 'Cafe Carnivale' presents a cabaret-style smorgasbord of authentic world music, from manic Balkan gypsy to Egyptian folk, all handpicked with dedication.

A range of culinary treats is available from the bar should you require a nibble to go with your Pinot mid-set; but remember to silence your phone once the door curtain has closed or you'll have the regulars baying for blood.

DANIEL BISHTON

> NIGHT OWL

Cnr City Rd & Cleveland St, Chippendale
(02) 9351 7940
www.seymour.usyd.edu.au/boxoffice/
soundlounge.shtml
Open Tues–Sat, licensed till 1am
Check website for upcoming shows
(generally on Friday and Saturday nights).

See also
map 2 D2

HOTEL HOLLYWOOD

LET'S DO THE TIME WARP

The day that Doris Goddard acquired the Hotel Hollywood, the clocks must have stopped: within the pub's Art Deco walls it has remained forever 1977. The carpet is blue and gaudy, the walls are dark-wood panelled, and a disco ball twirls lazily overhead. Miraculously spared during an epidemic of pub refits in the late 1990s and early 2000s, the Hollywood Hotel is a genie's bottle of retro charm on the fringe of Sydney's CBD.

It was spared, of course, thanks to the good taste of Doris herself, a singer and light entertainment starlet who appeared in films and on TV opposite the likes of Bob Hope and Peter Sellers. Next to the bar you'll find a collage of yellowing newspaper clippings from her 1950s heyday. She retired as publican a few years ago, but still lives on the premises and pops down to the bar occasionally to chat with regulars. Sometimes she even gets out her guitar and performs one of her own songs.

Located in a hub for the creative industries, the Hollywood boasts a clientele of actors*, models, graphic designers, journalists and assorted hipsters. Here they sit in cosy booths enjoying conversation, reasonably priced drinks and a hand-picked selection of live music. From Monday to Wednesday jazz combos perform, while Thursdays showcase indie bands and late-night blues. On Fridays and Saturdays there's no room for bands as the Hollywood is packed with punters, a cheerful crowd all adhering to the dress code as stated at the entrance: 'chips on shoulders must be left at the door.'

`NICK DENT`

> NIGHT OWL

2 Foster St, Surry Hills
(02) 9281 2765
www.hotelhollywood.com.au
Open Mon–Wed 12pm–12am,
Thurs–Fri 12pm–3am, Sat 5pm–3am

See also
map 1 B7

'ENCYCLO' TRIVIA

* One of Hugh Jackman's first movies, *Erskineville Kings* (1999), was filmed at the Hotel Hollywood.

> NIGHT OWL

LIFE'S NOT A DRAG AT THIS GAY CABARET

Queer Central at the Sly Fox Hotel in Sydney's inner west looks and feels pretty much like your typical non-descript boozer. That is until you suss out that it's gay cabaret night – the drag queens tottering on 12-inch heels at the bar and the Amy Winehouse look-alike canoodling with 'k.d. lang' in the corner are dead giveaways.

There's a mixed crowd here, with a large female contingent, who come to Queer Central to hang out, catch up, gossip, drink beer and take advantage of the 'free' pool table. This is also where you can see some of Sydney's leading drag queens, including Mitzi Macintosh, Sandi Hotrod and Bel West, strut their stuff while they verbalise their take on life and on the alternative Sydney scene. These pearls of wisdom come with laugh-out-loud dance routines, monologues and performance art.

Depending on who's performing, pick a pew and you might meet a drag queen wearing zebra-print thigh-high boots; a man (or a woman) in a blue, shiny lurex suit; or lesbian dancers wearing cowboy hats, nipple-tape tops, pink wigs and necklaces constructed from 7-inch vinyl records. With all this glamour who needs Oxford Street!

You'll probably want to go for a drink somewhere beforehand to get in the right mood, because Queer Central doesn't get going until after 10.30pm when the first show starts, and then around midnight all hell breaks loose.

JOANNA BOUNDS

> NIGHT OWL

Sly Fox Hotel,
199 Enmore Rd, Enmore
(02) 9557 1016
Free entry every Wed night with shows
starting 10.30pm & 11.30pm

See also
map 2 B3

'ENCYCLO' TRIVIA

* Known affectionately as the 'golden mile', Oxford Street, Darlinghurst, is the heart of Sydney's gay scene and home of the annual Sydney Gay and Lesbian Mardi Gras.

> NIGHT OWL

THE VICTORIA ROOM

COOL BRITANNIA

Sydney is known for its 'if you've got it, flaunt it' approach to promotion, so you could be forgiven for passing by the plain, brown doors of The Victoria Room on Darlinghurst's Victoria Street. Its nothing's-going-on-here entrance is definitely a mismatch with the opulence that lies within.

If you do venture beyond the heavy doors and up the stairs, you would be hard-pressed to believe that this inviting lounge, with its seductive orange glow, assortment of shabby chic antique sofas, rugs and tea lights, was once a bona fide car repair garage.

There are also touches of Indochine* in the bamboo curtains that separate the bar area from the restaurant. One of Sydney's very few late-night kitchens, The Victoria Room serves a supper menu between 11pm and 2am on Friday and Saturday nights – perfect for those with the munchies, who're after something other than a pizza or kebab. For those who prefer to eat earlier in the night, the restaurant menu, like the decor, is eclectic, mixing Italian antipasto plates with Moroccan meatballs and French desserts. And the prodigious list of cocktails will keep you occupied, with names like Hot Sugar Mama and Confused Romantic.

In keeping with its colonial charm, The Victoria Room is also the favoured afternoon destination for those who believe they were born in the wrong century. A silver-service high tea pops up on weekends, complete with tiered trays of finger sandwiches and scones with jam and cream.

If this was New York, you would need to bribe the door bitch to get in, but in Sydney you just need to have good taste and a preference for decadence without the showiness.   VALERIE KABOV

> NIGHT OWL

Level 1, 235 Victoria St, Darlinghurst
(02) 9357 4488
www.thevictoriaroom.com
Open Tues–Thurs 6pm–12am,
Fri 6pm–2am, Sat 12pm–2am,
Sun 1pm–12am; High Tea is served
Sat 12–5pm, Sun 1–5pm

See also
map 1 D7

'ENCYCLO' TRIVIA

* Indochine is a mixture of colonial French and Chinese styles from Indochina.

> NIGHT OWL

MOCEAN RESTAURANT AND UNDERGROUND BAR

WHAT LIES BENEATH

In the 1970s, The Astra Hotel was the beating heart of Bondi's sex, drugs and rock 'n' roll culture. Today the prominent Art Deco building is an eerily quiet retirement home that hides a well-kept secret. Go underground beneath the building and you'll find a flourishing little restaurant and bar where rock stars still come to let loose … sometimes.

Keep your eyes peeled, because you'll probably walk straight past Mocean (pronounced 'motion') if you don't know what to look for. From the outside all you'll see are the happy faces of patrons sitting at the outside tables sipping cocktails and people-watching. Inside, you'll find the restaurant with its Miami vibe, tropical-themed booths, hanging ferns, Chesterfield couch and huge screen print of a *Scarface*-era* Al Pacino.

The 'world menu' of generous tasting plates covers Mediterranean couscous, beetroot and goat's cheese salad, pan-fried barramundi wrapped in zucchini, and crispy soft shell crab.

But then there's the bar. Make your way down the winding staircase and, as your eyes adjust to the gentle lamplight, you'll see more smiley faces. Some perched on antique lounges; others nestled in lush velvet booths. Find yourself an intimate, dark corner and order a martini. Make friends and pick your favourite tunes from the retro jukebox. Have a little boogie when the DJ plays. But be warned: if 'special guests' arrive, the place is locked down and they party all night. Stars who've played impromptu sets here include the Pussy Cat Dolls, Foo Fighters and Dee Lite.

Get to Mocean by 6pm on Sunday for the scrumptious roast dinner plus funky beats on the decks upstairs and down. But shhhh … be quiet as you leave – you don't want to wake the neighbours. ANNA WARWICK

> NIGHT OWL

34A Campbell Pde, Bondi Beach
(02) 9300 9888
www.moceanbondi.com
Open Wed–Sun 6pm–12am

*See also
map 3 B2*

'ENCYCLO' TRIVIA

* *Scarface* (1983) is an epic crime drama in which Al Pacino stars as Tony Montana, a Cuban immigrant who takes over a Miami drug empire.

089

JUDGEMENT BAR

LAST DRINKS

One of the best ways to experience Sydney's night-owl scene is a schooner or two at the Courthouse Hotel's Judgement Bar. It's an unashamed drinking hole where people from all walks of life can finally let it all hang out – with no fear of being, well, judged.

You'll find the 'Judgey' at Taylor Square, the epicentre of Darlinghurst. Ignore the hotel's bar on the ground floor and head straight up the stairs to where the action is.

But don't get there too early. The Judgey is the kind of 24 hr down-and-dirty place where Sydneysiders bowl up at the end of the night because there's simply nowhere else open (definitely not a posh cocktail bar that you'd take a first date to!).

So, make sure you're suitably lubricated before you drop by, otherwise you'll fail to appreciate the bar's plastic tables and crazy clientele. Bag yourself a table (or metre of floor space) near one of the windows overlooking Oxford Street for the best spot to watch the partying gay boys, bright young things, trannies and working girls on the footpath below.

Then start chatting to your fellow drinker. They're the one sitting right next to you. They could well be a black-clad rock 'n' roll musician, bikie, street sweeper or fashion designer, or a clubber coming down after a night on the town. Before you know it, the sun will be rising, and you'll stumble out into the Sydney dawn to begin all over again.

JOANNA BOUNDS

> **NIGHT OWL**

Courthouse Hotel, Level 1, 189 Oxford St, Darlinghurst
(02) 9360 4831
www.courthousehotel.com.au
Open Mon–Wed 11.30am–10.30pm,
Thurs–Sun 24 hrs

See also
map 1 C8

your own sydney discoveries

photography credits

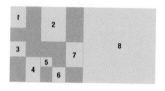

HIT THE STREETS

1. Courtesy of Sydney Harbour Kayaks
2. Ian Barry
3. Brett Boardman
4. Courtesy of Mu-Meson Archives
5. Courtesy of Clovelly Bowling Club
6. Courtesy of Conservation Volunteers Australia
7. Courtesy of Safe Surfing Schools
8. Frank Taylor

SYDNEY TRAPEZE SCHOOL

Photos by Frank Taylor

CAMPING ON COCKATOO ISLAND

Photo by Nerida McMurray

THE OLD FITZROY HOTEL

1. Martelle Hammar in *Sugarbomb* by Melita Rowston (Melita Rowston)
2. The Old Fitzroy Theatre with a full house (Dale)
3. Jay Ryan in *The Packer* by Diana Fuemana (Ian Barry)

SURFING IN MAROUBRA

Photo courtesy of Safe Surfing Schools

CLOVELLY BOWLING CLUB

Photos by Erika Budiman

SYDNEY THEATRE COMPANY BACKSTAGE TOURS

Photos by Brett Boardman

MU-MESON ARCHIVES

Photos courtesy of Mu-Meson Archives

CARRIAGEWORKS

1. Michael Nicholson
2.–3. Prue Upton

CONSERVATION VOLUNTEERS AUSTRALIA

Photos courtesy of Conservation Volunteers Australia

SYDNEY HARBOUR KAYAKS

Photo courtesy of Sydney Harbour Kayaks

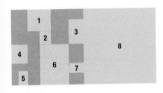

TREASURE TROVE

1. Courtesy of Glebe Markets
2. Courtesy of Wheels & Dollbaby
3. Fran Flynn @ Frangipani Creative
4. Courtesy of Mao & More

5. Chris Newport
6. Courtesy of Sydney Harbour Foreshore
7. Erika Budiman
8. Peter Coulson, Koukei Photography

MAO & MORE

Photos by Erika Budiman

BIRD TEXTILES EMPORIUM

1. & 5.–6. Courtesy of Bird Textiles Emporium
2., 4. & 7. Fran Flynn @ Frangipani Creative
3. Paul Henderson Kelly

FOOTAGE

1.–2. Erika Budiman
3. Chris Newport

GLEBE MARKETS

1.–2. & 4. Courtesy of Glebe Markets
3. Courtesy of RP's Hungarian Pastry
5. Erika Budiman

TITLE

Photo by Steve Kulak

GOULBURN & CROWN STREETS

1. Justin Smith
2.–4. & 6. Erika Budiman
5. & 7. Courtesy of Grandma Takes A Trip

GALLERY SERPENTINE

1. Peter Coulson, Koukei Photography
2.–3. Zelko Nedic, Ambo Ars Photography

ROKIT

1.–3. Erika Budiman
4. Courtesy of Sydney Harbour Foreshore

HAY STREET, HAYMARKET

1.–4. Erika Budiman
5. Garry Trinh

DIRTY PRETTY THINGS

Photos by Erika Budiman

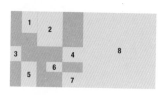

FEELING PECKISH?

1.–4. Erika Budiman
5. Sabine Albers
6. Courtesy of Gertrude & Alice Cafe Bookstore

7. Courtesy of Govinda's Restaurant and Movie Room
8. Kevin Low Photography

MAMAK
Photos by Kevin Low Photography

BODHI BAR
Photos by Erika Budiman

THE RUM DIARIES
Photos by Sabine Albers

DOMA BOHEMIAN BEER CAFE
Photos by Erika Budiman

CAFE ISH
Photos by Erika Budiman

GERTRUDE & ALICE CAFE BOOKSTORE
1. Courtesy of Gertrude & Alice Cafe Bookstore
2.–3. Erika Budiman

UCHI LOUNGE
Photos by Erika Budiman

BRAZUCA RESTAURANT & CHURRASCARIA
Photos courtesy of Brazuca Restaurant & Churrascaria

CORELLI'S CAFE GALLERY
Photos by Erika Budiman

GOVINDA'S RESTAURANT AND MOVIE ROOM
Photos courtesy of Govinda's Restaurant and Movie Room

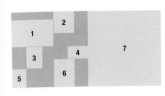

NIGHT OWL

1. Josh Clapp
2. Courtesy of The Victoria Room
3. Erika Budiman
4. Courtesy of Hotel Hollywood

5. & 7. Pete Kelly
6. Courtesy of Mocean Restaurant and Underground Bar

THE HOPETOUN HOTEL

Photo by Pete Kelly

HOTEL HOLLYWOOD

1. & 3. Courtesy of Hotel Hollywood
2. Dallas Kilponen

TIME TO VINO

1. & 3.–5. Erika Budiman
2. Courtesy of Time to Vino

QUEER CENTRAL

Photos by Erika Budiman

RUBY RABBIT

Photos by Josh Clapp

THE VICTORIA ROOM

Photos courtesy of The Victoria Room

CAFE HERNANDEZ

Photos by Erika Budiman

MOCEAN RESTAURANT AND UNDERGROUND BAR

Photos courtesy of Mocean Restaurant and Underground Bar

SOUND LOUNGE

Photos courtesy of Sound Lounge

JUDGEMENT BAR

Photo by Erika Budiman

ACKNOWLEDGEMENTS

The Publisher would like to acknowledge the following individuals and organisations:

Publications manager: Astrid Browne

Project manager: Melissa Krafchek

Editor: KJ Eyre

Design and photo selection: Erika Budiman

Writers: Nick Dent, Joanna Bounds, Denby Weller, Daniel Bishton, Ben Stubbs, Melinda Oliver, Anna Warwick, Valerie Kabov

Cartography: Emily Maffei

Pre-press: PageSet Digital Print & Pre-press

PHOTOGRAPHY CREDITS

Cover
Clockwise from main image:
A concentration of surfers at Bondi Beach (Rahul Dutta); Cocktail at The Victoria Room (Courtesy of The Victoria Room); *BabyLove* by ShuLea Cheang at CarriageWorks (Prue Upton); Edamame at Uchi Lounge (Erika Budiman); Gallery Serpentine outfit (Peter Coulson, Koukei Photography)

Back cover
Mosaic of female bather at Bondi Beach (Erika Budiman)

Half-title page
Mosaic of surfer on surfboard at Bondi Beach (Andrew Holt/Photographer's Choice/ Getty Images)

Title page
Sydney Harbour Bridge from Circular Quay train station (Erika Budiman)

About this guide
Eternity sign on pavement in Sydney (Erika Budiman)

Explore Australia Publishing Pty Ltd
85 High Street
Prahran, Victoria 3181, Australia

Published by Explore Australia Publishing Pty Ltd, 2009

Concept, text, maps, form and design © Explore Australia Publishing Pty Ltd, 2009

The maps in this publication incorporate data copyright © Commonwealth of Australia (Geoscience Australia), 2004. Geoscience Australia has not evaluated the data as altered and incorporated within this publication, and therefore gives no warranty regarding accuracy, completeness, currency or suitability for any particular purpose.

Inside front and back cover maps © Imprint and currency – VAR Product and PSMA Data

"Copyright. Based on data provided under licence from PSMA Australia Limited (www.psma.com.au)".

Hydrography Data (May 2006)
Parks & Reserves Data (November 2004)
Transport Data (February 2006)

DISCLAIMER

While every care is taken to ensure the accuracy of the data within this product, the owners of the data (including the state, territory and Commonwealth governments of Australia) do not make any representations or warranties about its accuracy, reliability, completeness or suitability for any particular purpose and, to the extent permitted by law, the owners of the data disclaim all responsibility and all liability (including without limitation, liability in negligence) for all expenses, losses, damages, (including indirect or consequential damages) and costs which might be incurred as a result of the data being inaccurate or incomplete in any way and for any reason.

ISBN 978 1 74117 287 4

10 9 8 7 6 5 4 3 2 1

Printed and bound in China by C & C Offset Printing Co. Ltd

Publisher's Note: Every effort has been made to ensure that the information in this book is accurate at the time of going to press. The publisher welcomes information and suggestions for correction or improvement. Email: info@exploreaustralia.net.au

Publisher's Disclaimers: The publisher cannot accept responsibility for any errors or omissions. The representation on the maps of any road or track is not necessarily evidence of public right of way. The publisher cannot be held responsible for any injury, loss or damage incurred during travel. It is vital to research any proposed trip thoroughly and seek the advice of relevant state and travel organisations before you leave.